PRAISE FOR THE BOOK

"If you want to have a meaningful conversation about finance with your bank, you need to talk their language. Take the time out to read this book and you'll be well equipped to have that conversation. A must-read for any business preparing its case for finance before meeting with their bank."

— Julio de Quesada, Independent Financial Services Professional; formerly Executive Vice President and Country Head, Citibank Mexico.

"An excellent roadmap for any business on how to develop and maintain an empathic relationship with its bank....written in a style which is easy to understand and offers valuable insights into the mindset of lending institutions."

— Eamonn Fitzgerald, Chief Executive, Hermitage Medical Clinic, Dublin, Ireland.

"As a first time successful owner of an SME for three and a half years this book is like reading déjà vu. A great reference guide on understanding how to analyse your business model, develop a persuasive case for finance and ensure success in securing funds for business growth in a new financial era."

— Steve Satherley, Owner, S & K Liquor, Wellington, New Zealand

"If finance is not your thing, then this book is for you! In less than 90 minutes, you'll be up to speed on what matters and what's needed to make a persuasive case for finance for your business. An excellent straight- talking read; I defy anyone to go through this book and not come away with a 'to do' list that improves their business case for finance."

— Joe Browne, Owner, SRXGlobal, Sydney, Australia

"I think we all know this stuff but never think about it from the banks perspective. We still deliver our business plans and wonder why banks don't seem to get it! A well written, informative guide to how the guys with the money think and what we as entrepreneurs need to focus on when looking for funding."

— Ian Searle, Managing Director, Talkis Limited, West Sussex, UK

To businesses that have it all,
except the money

DAVID SPARKS

THE QUICK GUIDE ON BUSINESS LOANS

WHAT YOU MUST KNOW BEFORE TALKING TO A BANK

First edition, 2013

Published by Deeno Publishing, MEDA House, Fielden Road, Crowborough, East Sussex TN6 1TP

ISBN: 978-0-9571322-1-4

Design, cover and layout by Ayd Instone, sunmakers.co.uk

Limits of Liability and Disclaimer of Warranty

The author of this book has used his best efforts in preparing this book. The author makes no representation or warranties with respect to the accuracy, applicability, fitness, or completeness of the contents of this book. The author disclaims any warranties (expressed or implied), merchantability, or fitness for any particular purpose. The author shall in no event be held liable for any loss or other damages, including but not limited to special, incidental, consequential, or other damages. As always, the advice of a competent legal, tax, accounting or other professional should be sought. The author does not warrant the performance, effectiveness or applicability of any sites listed in this book. All sites and links listed are for information purposes only and are not warranted for content, accuracy or any other implied or explicit purpose.

Published by Deeno Publishing, MEDA House, Fielden Road, Crowborough, East Sussex TN6 1TP, UK

Publisher's note

Every possible effort has been made to ensure that the information contained in this book is accurate at the time of going to press, and the publisher cannot accept responsibility for any errors or omissions, however caused. No responsibility for loss or damage occasioned to any person acting, or refraining from action, as a result of the material in this publication can be accepted by the editor or the publisher.

3 FREE BONUSES WAITING FOR YOU!

As a thank you for buying this book...

FREE BONUS №1

'If only I'd known what they would ask about my business, I wouldn't have stumbled so badly during the meeting...'
Don't let your bank give you any nasty surprises on the day.
Bonus No.1: Yes, I Want A Business Loan! – 107 Questions A Bank Will Ask Before Lending To You.

FREE BONUS №2

Bonus No.2 is a quality MP3 audio recording of this book.

FREE BONUS №3

Your copy of the Excel worksheets that detail all the financial calculations revealed in Secret No.5.

To receive ALL three free bonuses, go to the following web address: **www.financeandbanks.com/3bonuses** where you just need to give your name, email address and proof of purchase to receive all three bonuses TODAY!

P.S: I hate spam as much as you; I will never pass your details to anyone.

David Sparks

CONTENTS

"Business is really a profession often requiring for its practice quite as much knowledge, and quite as much skill, as law and medicine; and requiring also the possession of money."

— Walter Bagehot (1826 – 1877)

FOREWORD

Times have changed. Bank finance is no longer readily available. It is now a critical constraint for many businesses today. Many have difficulty renewing their existing credit facilities whilst other businesses report they cannot get business credit. Financial commentators report that the availability of finance is not going to get better any time soon.

With finance being effectively rationed, a business must do all it can to place itself at the front of the queue. Businesses have to create and deliver persuasive and compelling sales pitches to their banks; pitches that are as persuasive and compelling as those they create for marketing their products and services. They must know what their banks want to hear and be able to present their case using language that bank managers understand.

That's what this book is about. David Sparks takes the reader inside the mind of a commercial bank manager, revealing what every business must know before they sit down in front of their bank manager to negotiate new credit facilities or the renewal of existing credit facilities.

This book is much more than just another read on business finance: it is a practical and revealing guide for anyone in business to help create a strong case for finance today and secure a future for their business tomorrow.

— Jonathan Jay
Founder & Chairman,
The Nationwide Alliance of Business Owners
www.nabo.biz

THE SECRETS ARE OUT

You don't need me or anyone else to tell you that the availability of finance for small businesses has taken a sharp fall since the banking crisis in 2008. You know that already. And for those who do manage to get their hands on the finance that they need to start or stay in business, the cost of that finance is getting more expensive.

Unfortunately, for reasons I will not bore you with right now, total bank lending is not going to increase any time soon, in spite of politicians around the world pleading with the banks to do so. There will continue to be winners and losers when it comes to getting business finance for the foreseeable future.

The sad irony is that world economies today are more dependent than ever on the ability of businesses to survive and prosper. The future depends, more than ever, on the ingenuity and perseverance of private enterprise to create wealth and restore economic growth.

Helping business owners to grow their businesses is not only good for them; it is also good for the people they employ and good for the economic and social well being of society as a whole.

My guess, though, is that you are just too busy running your existing business to be thinking about how a bank decides if you get the finance or not.

This is precisely why I've written this book: to share with you exactly what you must know about:

- *how banks think*
- *what banks want to hear, and*
- *the information that supports favourable lending decisions*

I cannot guarantee that you will actually get the finance you need for your business after reading this book. I am certain, though, that action you can take based on the information in the pages that follow will help you make a persuasive case for finance; one that, I hope, is successful and helps realise the dreams that you have for your business.

Let's jump straight in.

David Sparks.

SECRET № 1

ON CUSTOMERS, MARKET SHARE AND COMPETITION

How's business?

The temptation might be to say that it's just fine if only the bank would lend the money you need to keep going. And if they'd just say yes, like they say they do in the commercials, you could be in and out of there in ten minutes flat. This approach may have worked when banks were falling over themselves to lend; it's not working anymore.

Many existing businesses struggle to make a successful pitch to their banks. New businesses have a particularly tough time of it. High street banks, in their desire to see a business track record, are often unwilling to consider finance for a new kid on the block.

Let's not beat around the bush. If you are someone with a great idea looking for finance to take it to the next stage, then you will probably need to talk to a financial service organisation other than a bank. Banks are not venture capitalists; they are not organisations that fund experimental research on products that are untested in the market place.

What is true, though, is that you, as a business owner or business manager must be ready to spell out exactly what your business is and why a bank or other financing organisation is making a smart decision to put their money on the table. A solid business plan is the first step to achieve this end. I'm not referring here to a document that is carefully written, bound, filed away safely and cherished for ever more. A real business plan is a living piece of work; something that must be kept alive and relevant, refined and updated regularly to take account of constantly changing conditions, threats and opportunities for your business*.

Who are your customers?

I'm not a big fan of smart sounding phrases but make an exception here. Whatever your business is, you must be ready to make the case as to exactly why the customers you are targeting will buy what you are selling. You must, in other words, have a Unique Selling Proposition. And since that's a bit of a mouthful, most refer to it as a USP.

A USP is something that allows you to say that the product or service that you've got is different from what your competition is selling. Your business must first, though, have a crystal clear idea of, exactly, whom it is selling to; so let's talk about that first.

Let's say your business is selling mountain bikes. Your potential customer base might be anyone over the age of 12 with a desire to take exercise. That's a big potential customer base. It's also, from a marketing point of view, a very poorly defined customer base. There is a risk in marketing to a poorly defined customer base: the risk is that in the hope of trying to appeal to everyone, you end up appealing to no one.

So let's try again.

We could focus on young adults aged up to 25, who are fashion conscious, health conscious & live in the countryside. Or maybe focus on older adults: those over 35 years of age who did some cycling when they were younger and now want to get back on their bikes.

In each case, how you appeal to these different customer segments is different. When profiling your perfect customer, it helps to think of someone you know that you would consider a perfect customer for your product or service.

And then ask yourself, how you might reach more people just like that person. Each customer segment has a unique customer profile. So, for each customer segment, you need a well defined marketing strategy that specifies how you will reach those customers.

The bonus is that the customers you actually get from such targeted marketing are not only those that satisfy the particular profiles, but also those that identify themselves with the profile of the customer that you are actually marketing to. Some older adults, for instance, in their perception that they are forever young, respond to the marketing efforts actually directed at younger adults. And that, of course, is fine!

** Although a lot of what we talk about in this book will be found in a business plan, this book is not about business planning or how to go about putting a business plan together. See the Further Reading section for some reccommended titles.*

Why market share matters

You can only begin to think about your potential market after defining your customer profiles. And the better you profile your prospective customers, the better you can define your potential market. If your business has no competition, that's great! Most, though, operate in markets where they must compete with others for business.

Defining your market means having to work out how many fashion and health conscious adults aged up to 25 there are in your area or how many 35+ adults there are who cycled when they were younger.

This requires an investment of your time in order to research the demographics of the city or region where your business is located. It's important to keep an open mind when you do this. You may well find that there are greater opportunities by targeting a different segment of the market.

A bank expects you to know and talk knowledgably about:

- The size of your market(s)
- How your business stacks up against the competition
- What share of the market your business has today, and
- What your projected market share is in the coming six to twelve months

It's not just how well your business is doing that matters but, also, how well your business is doing compared to your competition. If your business is growing at 10%, that may sound fine until you learn that the industry that your business is in is growing at 25%.

A bank is likely to have other customers in a similar or competing business as your own and will complete its market analysis for your business based not only on information that you provide but also using their knowledge of your market from other sources.

Banks get nervous when they see a business with a small market share. They know that such businesses often get undercut on price because a larger competing business can survive on lower profit margins. If a competing business has a greater market share, a bank figures that unless your business has a USP, there's a real risk that you may not survive in the longer term.

You must have a realistic view of your potential market. Don't fall into the trap of defining your market too loosely and then concluding that your current share of that market is very small. It is far better to define your business market more tightly and emphasize the unique position and more substantial potential market share that your business plans to have in that better defined market.

What we're really saying here is that there's no substitute for investing your time in market research for whatever it is you are selling. There are organisations that offer market research services to new and established businesses that may be worth checking out. Just to give you an idea, have a look at www.marketest.co.uk.

What to remember

- ✓ Your business plan is a living document; once prepared, it must be revisited on a regular basis and kept up to date with the latest vision and plans for your business.
- ✓ Banks are not venture capitalists. They want to see that your business has a proven track record of generating cash before they will consider credit facilities.
- ✓ You must have a crystal clear idea of whom you are selling to; so clear that you can pick out potential customers walking down a street.
- ✓ Be prepared to talk to a bank about the customer profiles that your business is actively reaching out to and the marketing strategies to reach new customers.
- ✓ Be ready to talk to a bank about the market for your business: the absolute size of your clearly defined market, the current market share in that market and your business strategy to grow your market share.
- ✓ The better you define the specific customer market that you are selling your product or service to, the more focused you will be in your marketing efforts and the greater the chance that your business will be successful.

SECRET № 2

WHY PROFITS DO NOT IMPRESS A BANK AS MUCH AS CASH

Must your business show a profit to get finance?

The answer surprises some people. A business making a loss can qualify for finance. To understand why this is the case, let's talk about profit and loss numbers for a moment.

The amount of profit or loss for a business depends on the accounting rules used when calculating that profit or loss. I know you may feel like switching off at the mention of accounting; but stick with me, I'll be very brief. The point here is this:

Different accounting rules give different profit and loss numbers.

Let's put that another way – there's no right or wrong number for a profit or loss calculation:

- If the accounting rules are reasonable, then the reported profit or loss number is reasonable.
- If the accounting rules are not reasonable, the reported profit or loss is not a fair reflection of how well or badly a business is doing.

The poor state of Enron's financial health was hidden from view because the accounting rules used in calculating its reported income were far from reasonable. Enron's reported profit were based on devious tricks to show profits that, we all subsequently found out, did not exist at all. So if profit is not a "must have" in the eyes of a bank, what is? The answer is cash flow.

Why cash matters more than profits

When a bank looks at a set of business forecasts, there's one forecast in particular that's of interest to them over all others. And that's the cash forecast. Although banks expect you to have a sales forecast indicating when you expect to sell your products or services, what they are really interested in is when you collect the money from the sales of those products or services.

You see income statements (also known as profit and loss accounts) suffer from, what I call, the Potential Fatal Flaw:

Income statements are prepared on the assumption that a business collects the cash owing from its customers.

The impact of the Potential Fatal Flaw varies from business to business. If you are, for instance, running a grocery store it will not bother you. Why? Because customers in your grocery store are cash customers; they pay you in cash or use a credit or debit card at the time of sale.

But let's say that instead of a grocery store, you own and run a computer services company. You offer two months credit to your business customers as you know if you don't, there's a real chance that your customers will take their business elsewhere. In this case, assuming the price at which you sell your computer services covers all your costs, you will show a profit in your income statement.

The big difference, compared to the grocery store, is that you run the risk that some of your customers may not pay you before the end of your "two months to pay" credit policy. It's not that your customers don't want to pay you. They may just need more time and delay their payment to you for as long as they can to help manage their own cash flows.

If you find out, however, that a customer is in real financial trouble, and there's a strong possibility that the customer may never pay you, that's a different story. In this case the accounting rules require that you remove from your books the computer service fees you already recorded as income over two months ago. This is done by recording an expense in your books called a provision for bad debts.

Let's think about this for a moment.

What we're saying is that the income (and therefore the profits) your computer service company recorded two months earlier were too big or, in bank language, were overstated:

The income and profits were recorded on the assumption that the service fees due would be collected in the future.

And this is exactly what happens in real life: businesses report profits relating to services provided for which they have not yet been paid; their customers get into financial difficulties and the business ends up having to make an adjustment to sales that were booked earlier but must now be reversed. This is one reason why businesses reporting profits can have cash flow problems.

Let's think of it this way: the recorded profit number for any business that has sales on credit may need to be revised in the future. That possibility of a future revision to a reported profit number makes a profit number, what I call, a soft number.

Let's compare a profit number with a number for the amount of cash in a business. Unlike a profit number, there's no assumption behind a number for cash. The amount of cash can be easily checked. If the cash is $5,000* on a particular date, it can be readily verified by looking at the businesses' bank statement – either the business has the $5,000 or it doesn't. A number for cash is a hard number.

Don't get me wrong. I'm not saying that a bank doesn't care if you make a profit or not. Clearly in the long run you're in business to make a profit. It is obviously better to be able to show a track record of profits rather than a track record of losses!

**The $ currency sign is used throughout this book for convenience only; feel free to replace it with the currency in your life.*

If, though, a business keeps reporting losses it will eventually run out of cash unless more cash is continually found to pump into such a business to keep it afloat. And that's not a compelling business proposition.

The point is this: a loss-making business today that has a solid plan for return to profitability and is supported with realistic cash flow projections sufficient to justify the finance requested is something that an experienced commercial banker should be prepared to consider.

It's the health of your future cash flows that matter

Banks, of course, are aware of the Potential Fatal Flaw. Banks know well that there's a big difference between selling something and getting paid for selling something. They are much more interested in knowing when your business will collect the money from the sale than when you make the sale itself.

Banks understand that your ability to service and repay any lending depends on the health of the cash flow of your business, not on its profitability. This is why the focus is always on your cash forecast (also known as projected cash flow) and not your sales forecast.

It's one thing to prepare a cash flow forecast. It's quite another to convince a bank your forecast is realistic and achievable. Banks know that a business never goes bankrupt in its forecasts. This is precisely the reason banks will tend to start from the position that your forecasts err on the optimistic side. Any business forecast is only as good as the business assumptions used in preparing the forecast. It's the assumptions behind the numbers that receive close scrutiny by a bank. A bank takes a very close look at the assumptions on which your cash forecast is based. It's down to you to convince them that the assumptions on which your cash forecast is based are reasonable and appropriate.

Banks use something called sensitivity analysis to test the assumptions in your business forecasts. This analysis gives a bank an indication of the ability of your business to service borrowings under varying business conditions. We cover exactly what sensitivity analysis is and how a bank uses it later.

What you need to know

- ✓ A loss making business does not necessarily have cash flow problems. A business that makes losses can survive; a business that runs out of cash is fighting for survival.
- ✓ A business making profits can find itself fighting for survival if it is failing to collect money due from customers to whom the business has extended credit.
- ✓ Banks focus on future cash flows for your business to assess your business' ability to service and repay new borrowings.
- ✓ If your business is running at a loss when you are looking for finance, you must have a convincing plan to get back to profitability.
- ✓ Your plan must be supported by realistic cash flow projections that will be more than sufficient to meet the repayments for the finance requested.

SECRET № 3

THE LINK BETWEEN CAPITAL, PROFITS AND CASH REVEALED

How do you put money into your business?

There are two basic choices when it comes to putting your own money into your business:

- Lend your money to your business or
- Put your money into your business as capital (also known as equity capital).

There's a big difference.

If you lend your money, it means that your business should pay that money back to you at some point in the future.

Putting your money in as capital sends an entirely different message to a bank. In this case your money is in the business for the long term. Banks prefer to see your money in your business as long term capital rather than just lent to your business.

Assuming your business does well, it will make a profit. Profit increases the amount of capital in your business. You, as the owner, then decide if those profits are to be reinvested in your business. If not reinvested, the withdrawal of profit is a reduction in the total capital in your business.

On the other hand, if your business makes losses, then there are no profits to add to the existing capital. In this case, the total amount of capital will decrease because of the losses.

So, at any time, the total capital or the total net worth of your business is made up of:

- paid-in capital,
- plus profits of the business that are kept in the business,
- less any losses made by the business.

A business is solvent when the total net worth is a positive number. It's therefore possible for a business to make some losses but to remain solvent.

If, however, the total losses over time are greater than the paid in capital and any profits kept in the business, then the net worth of the business would be a negative number; in this case the business would be insolvent. It should be no surprise to you that banks have a strong preference for solvent businesses.

How a bank thinks about capital, profits and cash

Let's assume your business has done well over the last three years; it has made profits and kept those profits in its expanding business. The amount of total profits invested in the business, therefore, get larger as the years go by. The net worth of your business will have increased year after year.

As profits do not have to be kept in the business for the long term, profits are, in accountant-speak, available for distribution: the profits are available to be taken out of the business at any time.

But there's a catch.

We saw earlier that it's possible for a business to show a profit whilst at the same time have no cash. So, can an owner take profits out of the business when there is no cash in the business bank account?

Answer: No, the owner cannot.

The point is this: A business must have the cash and net accumulated profits before it can take money out of the business as dividends or drawings.

A business has net accumulated profits when the total profits made and kept in that business are greater than any losses made since the start of that business. If losses are greater than the profits since the start of a business, then that business would have net accumulated losses.

Remember that an owner receives a salary for his work as a director or employee in his own business. This is recorded as a business expense. Dividends or drawings, on the other hand, are not business expenses; they are a distribution of profits made by the business to the owner.

Consider the following case:

The owner of a successful business has run into cash flow difficulties and decides he must ask his bank for an increase in the existing approved business credit facility. The owner explains to the bank that it's a short term cash flow need as business always slows down at this time of year.

The financials for the business indicate that the business has been profitable during the last three years and that there is $100,000 of profits already earned and reinvested in the business along with the original paid-in capital of $20,000. There is $1,000 in the business bank account at the time of the meeting with the bank. The business owner asks for $20,000 to be made available for six months. The bank does its due diligence and satisfies itself that the money would be put to good use by the business.

Both the bank and the owner understand that the additional cash flow the business must generate to service and repay the proposed new borrowings of $20,000 will only be made by the business if the money borrowed is actually invested in the business.

The question is this: if the bank decides to approve the temporary increase of $20,000 in the existing business credit facility for general purpose use, what could the business owner actually do with that money?

Answer: Anything the owner wants. The owner could use the $20,000 to go on a well-deserved holiday!

The fact is that a bank has little or no control over how money is actually spent once the lending has been approved. Let me qualify that last sentence. A bank could monitor a customer's account from day to day and question all withdrawals of cash or transfers out of the account that do not appear to be for a business purpose. In practise, though, such real time monitoring of customers does not take place.

Although the business owner commits that the funds are for business use, there is, in theory, little to stop the owner from paying for a holiday once the increase in the credit facility has been approved and is available for use. Our friend may enjoy his snorkelling holiday but it will be the last one he goes on for a while!

The essential point is that any banking relationship is founded on trust. A banks' homework, when approving a loan facility, includes making a judgement on whether they really trust you or not. If a bank decides it does not trust you, you're not getting the finance no matter how attractive your business proposition is.

There is one other approach the business, looking for the $20,000, could take that would help a bank sleep better at night. It could do the legal paperwork necessary to commit some or all of the $100,000 profits already earned by the business as long term capital. Accountants have a fancy term for this: they call it capitalisation of earnings. This is a process by which profits are converted into long term capital and are, then, no longer available for distribution as dividends or drawings to the owner.

The reclassification of profits as long term capital is a positive signal to a bank that an owner is committed to their business for the long term.

If you decide that you do not want to put your money in as capital but, instead, only lend your money to your business, a bank is likely to require you to subordinate your loan to any bank debt in your business. In this case the money you lend to your business can only be legally repaid to you after the bank debt is repaid.

A bank could consider treating a loan to your business as quasi equity capital when doing their credit review if it is completely satisfied that you, as the owner, will leave those funds permanently in your business. In practise though, a bank will much prefer that you commit the funds to your business by investing those funds as capital for the long term.

Working capital: what it is and why it matters

So far we've only talked about capital as money invested by an owner in a business. Now is a good time to introduce another type of capital: working capital.

Do you remember that computer services business that you were running? Well, one of your close friends, Stingray, noticed that your business was doing well and has decided to give you some competition by starting his own computer services business.

Stingray, no longer a close friend, is investing $20,000 in his business; $10,000 is his own money and the other $10,000 borrowed from his Aunt Agatha. This $20,000 is needed to rent business premises, lease a commercial van and purchase Macs, PCs and computer accessories for resale.

In order to attract some customers away from your business, he is offering three months credit. This means that, at any point in time, Stingray will have customers that owe him about three months worth of sales, assuming they take the three month credit terms and assuming they pay him on time.

So what's Stingray's working capital? Well, it's simply a calculation on a particular date of how much money is tied up in his business.

Here's one way to think about it:

Stingray will always have to have some Macs, PCs and computer accessories in stock and, because his business sells on credit, there will always be money owed by customers to the business. The amount of inventory (also referred to as stock) together with the amount owed by customers at any point in time are assets on the books. They represent monies tied up in the business that need to be financed.

When Stingray buys Macs and PCs from his suppliers on credit, the business then owes money to the suppliers. The amount owed is recorded as a liability by the business: "amount owed to suppliers". The fact that Stingray's business does not pay its supplier immediately is a source of finance.

So back to the original question:

The term working capital is a calculation on a particular date of how much is tied up in the business. The calculation itself is straight forward: it's the amount of your short term business assets (that is, inventory and amounts owed to you by customers). And from that total you subtract your short term business liabilities (amounts owed to suppliers).

Here's what you need to know: when your business is growing, the amount of inventory in your store or warehouse, and the amount of cash that customers owe you are also growing. Your business needs finance to fund that growth.

The actual amount of working capital finance you need is the total of these short term business assets less the amount your business owes to its suppliers.

The general rule is that as a business grows, its need for working capital finance grows.

In addition to the need for working capital finance, sufficient cash must be available to pay wages, salaries and other operating expenses.

A business also needs finance for investment in business premises, equipment, machinery and other assets not for resale but for use in the business. This type of investment is known as capital expenditure. It's this type of expenditure that is reported as fixed assets on the balance sheet for a business.

It's important to realise that it is not necessary to buy many assets for use by a business. Many chose to lease furniture, equipment and machinery rather than buy such assets outright. It is certainly better from a cash flow perspective. The lease vs. buy decision is a well trodden path. The chapter 'Finance from organisations other than banks' details financial service organisations and intermediaries that offer commercial leasing as an alternative to outright purchase.

What you need to remember

- ✓ Banks favour businesses with long term capital.
- ✓ A business must have the cash and reported profits before it can take money out of the business as dividend or drawings to pay to the owner.
- ✓ A bank may have a concern where a significant portion of total capital is profits available for distribution to the owner. One risk, in a bank's mind, is that incremental borrowings could be taken out of the business by the owner instead of being invested in the business.
- ✓ Businesses can reclassify their profits as long term capital. By doing so, those profits are no longer available for distribution as drawings or dividends. This action is reassuring to a bank as it indicates the owner is committed to his or her business.
- ✓ A growing business is likely to have a financing need for capital expenditure and working capital finance.
- ✓ A business needs the use of fixed assets, not necessarily to own them. Leasing is often a viable and sensible alternative to the outright purchase of fixed assets.
- ✓ The amount of working capital finance required depends upon the growth in inventory, growth in amounts owed by customers and growth in credit from suppliers.

Notes

SECRET №

4

HOW A BANK EVALUATES YOUR BUSINESS

Why your credit report matters

> Meeting with a bank to discuss finance for your business without knowing what your credit report says about you is not a smart idea.

A review of your personal credit profile and your business credit profile (if your business has a credit profile) is a critical step by any bank when evaluating your application for finance. For small business financing, the personal credit profile matters a lot as there is often no business credit rating available.

Whilst this credit checking should come as no surprise, many do not take the time to check their credit report and credit score prior to initial discussions with their bank. Credit reporting and credit scoring are competitive businesses and, for this reason, there are organisations online to help get the information that you need. You may, in fact, find that some information on your credit report is incorrect and negatively impacting your credit score. Credit report agencies include:

www.experian.com,
www.experian.co.uk,
www.equifax.com,
www.equifax.co.uk and
www.creditreport.com.

The message is clear: banks will always require bank references and credit references. So check your credit before you talk to a bank. If the credit rating is not what you expect, find out why and what steps you can take to improve your credit rating. If your rating is not strong, be prepared to explain to a bank why it is not a true reflection of your credit worthiness.

How a bank thinks about the credit decision

Let's assume that a bank has decided, in principle, to consider offering finance to your business. The bank's first thought, like it or not, is how it's going to get its money back! The rule that a bank uses here is that there should be at least two "ways out" of any lending deal. They want to see two ways that the debt repayments will come from your business.

The first and expected way out is from your business cash flows: your business cash forecasts need to show that sufficient operating cash flow will be generated to pay the additional debt costs. Banks like to see the debt burden decreasing as time goes by in your financial forecasts.

The second way out for a bank, if the first way out fails, might be the required transfer of business assets to the bank. The bank, for instance, might agree to finance a business asset such as a piece of machinery on the understanding that the bank has the right to take possession of the machinery if your business fails to generate sufficient cash to meet the debt repayment terms.

In this case, the bank's second way out might be to take ownership of the machinery and then arrange for the sale of this machinery. The proceeds from the sale of the machinery would be used to reduce the amount your business owes to the bank. This is clearly not a pleasant situation to be in for any business.

There are other business assets that are more attractive to a bank than physical assets as a second way out. An example of such assets is amounts due from your customers (also known as trade receivables or trade debtors). For its second way out, a bank could take, what's called, a floating charge over such receivables. This means if your business fails to meet the debt repayments when they fall due, the bank has the right to collect the monies that are due from your customers.

So, if you are the bank, what type of asset might you prefer to receive as a second way out? A physical asset (like a cement mixer)? Or financial assets, like amounts owed by your customers?

Here's the reality: banks have little appetite for holding, what they call, non-earning assets on their balance sheet. Physical assets such as cement mixers and machinery are non-earning assets: they sit on a bank's balance sheet and do not earn anything.

Taking ownership of plant, equipment or commercial vehicles and trying to subsequently sell such assets at a decent price is actually a hassle for banks. Even non-earning assets that have a ready market (such as repossessed property) are often sold off by banks at attractive prices just to get them off the books.

The fact is that it's much easier to collect receivables from customers. After all, receivables are just cash waiting to be collected. And that's seen as a good thing by banks. Unlike an ageing cement mixer, receivables are usually liquid assets. They represent recent sales to customers that bought on credit. Receivables are constantly renewed as customers buy on credit, pay and then buy on credit again. Receivables are, for this reason, known as self-liquidating financial assets.

It should come as no surprise that a bank likes self-liquidating financial assets. It's worth noting, though, that any floating charge over business assets agreed is likely to be for greater than the amount owing by the business to the bank. This is because, practically speaking, a business will likely be already in trouble at the time its bank is looking to the floating charge as its way out. By that time, the uncollected business receivables are likely to be made up of amounts owing that have been difficult to collect; also, the resale value of unsold inventory that is still in the warehouse is likely to have fallen as word has spread that the business is in trouble. This is why a bank will normally give itself a cushion by requiring a floating charge over business assets with a value well in excess of the amount owed to the bank.

We said earlier that banks look for at least two ways out. A third way out is often a request by the bank for a personal guarantee. Many business owners are rightly slow to pledge personal assets. It does, however, send a strong message of commitment to a business when such guarantees are provided by business owners.

You might well ask if a bank accepts business assets as security and receives personal guarantees when they provide finance, why should they care if your business is successful or not?

The truth is that banks do have a vested interest in the success of your business: in the long term, it's only as your business grows, that a banks' business grows. This is precisely the reason why a business will not get finance just because it offers security or personal financial guarantees. A bank expects to be repaid from the cash flow of a business, not from the forced sale of business assets or from calling on financial guarantees.

How a bank decides on the credit rating for your business

All businesses need systems: systems for production, for sales, for payroll and so on. Banks are no different. And the system or process that banks use to decide which customers get the bank's money is called the Credit Approval Process.

Just like Colonel Sanders has his secret recipe for his Kentucky Fried Chicken®, banks have their own secret recipes for working out if they should lend to your business or not.

For existing businesses, banks expect to receive audited financial statements for the last two or three years as well as other internal financial reports and projections that management uses to run the business. This information is fed into a bank's internal credit rating model.

So, what information is held in a bank's credit rating model? Well, it's not rocket science. The model does a few things:

- It produces your actual & forecast numbers in a standard format. This process is known by those working in banking as the spreading of financials.

- It also calculates and stores different types of financial ratios for your business.

For example, the Net Income to Sales ratio is Net Income divided by Sales. The result is multiplied by 100 to make it a percentage. This particular ratio is a measure of the profitability of the products or services that your business sells.

Not all financial ratios, however, are born equal. Some ratios are much more relevant than others when it comes to deciding on the appropriate credit rating for a business.

The financial ratios that really matter when a bank works out an appropriate credit rating for your business are those that measure:

- **how well your business manages its liquidity**; in other words, how well inventory, trade receivables and trade payables (also known as trade creditors) are managed (LIQUIDITY RATIOS),
- **the amount of existing debt in your business** (EXTENT OF DEBT RATIOS), and
- **the health of the cash flow in your business** (CASH FLOW RATIOS)

The assessment of the credit attractiveness of your business is based on the output from the banks' internal credit rating model. This model ranks the risk of a loan on something like a one to ten scale; a scale that is linked to a statistical probability of default and probability of loss in the event of default.

The more creditworthy a business is - measured by low leverage, high debt coverage and healthy liquidity - the better its credit risk rating will be. And the better its credit risk rating is, the more attractive the terms, conditions and pricing of credit is likely to be.

In Secret No.5 we look in detail at each of the financial ratios that really matter, showing how each one is calculated and what each one means. We also take a close look at some other financial ratios that are taken into account by a bank: ratios that measure the operational efficiency and profitability of a business.

What to remember

- ✓ Know what's in your credit report and your credit score before you meet with the bank.
- ✓ A banks' credit rating assessment is a measurement of the perceived risk of your business as a potential borrower of the bank's money.
- ✓ Banks look for at least two "ways out" when doing a business loan evaluation; the first from business cash flow, the second from transfer of business assets to the bank.
- ✓ A third "way out" is often personal financial guarantees provided by the owner based on their personal net worth.
- ✓ Personal guarantees indicate a high level of commitment by the owner to their bank.
- ✓ The financial ratios that really matter in a bank's credit rating assessment are those that measure the liquidity, the extent of existing debt and the health of the cash flow in your business.
- ✓ Other ratios that measure the profitability and operational efficiency of your business are also taken into account.

Notes

SECRET № 5

LOOK AT YOUR NUMBERS THE SAME WAY A BANK DOES

Financial ratios that really matter

> Some feel a sudden tiredness coming on at the mention of the words 'financial analysis' or, worse still, 'financial ratios'. If you happen to fall into this category, have a strong coffee before proceeding any further. The unfortunate reality is that your bank manager expects you to display an understanding of the financial mechanics of your business. The good news is that getting a handle on the meaning of the numbers for your business is not rocket science at all.

Key financial ratios that a bank will review when rating the creditworthiness of your business are:

Liquidity ratios:

- *Current Ratio:* a measure of how easily your business can meet its short term obligations; the higher the ratio the better.

- *Quick Ratio:* a tougher measure of the liquidity of your business than the Current Ratio; the higher the ratio the better.

Extent of Debt ratios:

- *Leverage Ratio:* a measure of the extent of debt in a business. Some debt is good; too much debt usually results in cash flow problems.

- *Interest Cover:* a measure of how big interest expense is when compared to net income; generally, the higher the ratio the better.

Cash Flow ratios:

- *Fixed Charge Cover:* a measure of the ability of a business to cover 'must pay' expenses (more on what we mean by this later); the higher the better.

- *Cash Flow to Total Debt %*: a measure of the capacity of a business to generate cash by comparing cash flow with the total debt in the business.

The following table shows the formulae used to calculate each of these ratios:

Financial ratios that really matter

Ratio	Formula
Liquidity Ratios	
Current Ratio	Current Assets / Current Liabilities
Quick Ratio	Current Assets – Inventory / Current Liabilities
Extent of Debt Ratios	
Leverage Ratio %	Total Liabilities X 100 / Owners Equity
Interest Cover	Net Income + interest expense / Interest expense
Cash Flow Ratios	
Fixed Charge Cover	Net Income+interest+rent paid+depreciation / Interest + rent paid
Cash Flow to Total Debt %	(Net Income + Depreciation) X 100 / Total Debt

Let's take a look at Aroma Manufacturing, an existing business that produces natural food flavourings for sale to food manufacturers. Here are Aroma's summary income statements and balance sheets for the last three years:

Aroma's Financial Statements

Income Statement		**20X3**		**20X2**		**20X1**
Sales		$12,500		$7,000		$3,000
Cost of Goods Sold		8,750		4,900		2,100
Gross Income		3,750		2,100		900
Interest expense	**250**		**50**		-	
Depreciation	**450**		**220**		**130**	
Other expenses	1,800		1,480		1,370	
Total Expenses		2,500		1,750		1,500
Net Income		**$1,250**		**$350**		**$ (600)**
Balance Sheet						
Fixed Assets						
Land & Buildings		$1,500		$500		-
Plant, Machinery, Cars		2,500		1,000		650
		4,000		1,500		650
Current Assets						
Inventory	**1,650**		**750**		**300**	
Trade Receivables	2,350		900		350	
Cash at bank	-		100		300	
	4,000		**1,750**		**950**	
Current Liabilities						
Trade Payables	1,200		600		200	
Short term bank loan	**300**		-		-	
	1,500		**600**		**200**	
Net Current Assets		2,500		1,150		750
		$6,500		$2,650		$1,400
Financed by						
Paid In Capital		$2,000		$2,000		$2,000
Retained Income, 1 Jan	(250)		(600)		0	
Current year income	1,250		350		(600)	
Retained Income, 31 Dec		1,000		(250)		(600)
Equity (Owners Investment)		**3,000**		**1,750**		**1,400**
Long Term Debt		**3,500**		**900**		**0**
		$6,500		$2,650		$1,400

Before we go any further, I want to make clear that we have absolutely no interest in understanding (and we do not need to understand) the weird looking format that accountants use to present the financial position of a business. The only reason we are showing the financial statements above is so that you have some idea of where the numbers come from for the straight forward calculations we are about to do. The numbers we use from Aroma's financial statements in calculating the ratios that appear in the following table are highlighted in **bold**.

Aroma's ratios that really matter

	20X3	20X2	20X1
Liquidity Ratios			
Current Ratio	2.7	2.9	4.8
Quick Ratio	1.6	1.7	3.3
Extent of Debt Ratios			
Leverage Ratio %	167%	86%	14%
Interest Cover	6.0	8.0	-
Cash Flow Ratios			
Fixed Charge Cover	7.8	12.4	-
Cash Flow to Total Debt %	45%	63%	-

The Current Ratio for 20X1, for example, is $950 divided by $200 = 4.8.

The Quick Ratio for the same year is ($950 minus $300) divided by $200 = 3.3.

The Leverage Ratio % for 20X1 is ($200 + $ nil) divided by $1,400 multiplied by 100 = 14%.

As there was no interest expense in 20X1, Interest Cover is a meaningless calculation for that year. In 20X2, however, Aroma did take on some bank debt and the Interest Cover is calculated as ($350 + $50) divided by $50 = 8.

Fixed Charge Cover for 20X2 is ($350 + $50 + $220) divided by $50 = 12.4.

Finally, Cash Flow to Total Debt % for 20X2 is ($350 + $220) divided by $900 multiplied by 100 = 63%.

What's infinitely more important, though, than doing all these calculations is to understand if they are good or bad news. So let's talk through them.

1. The Current Ratio

The Current Ratio is a crude measure that indicates if the business is liquid or not. The terms "current assets" and "current liabilities", invented by accountants, are used in the calculation and deserve an explanation.

Current assets refer to assets that mature in less than one year. Trade receivables are normally a current asset as amounts owed by credit customers will normally be due for payment well within one year. If Aroma's business is offering 90 days credit terms and all customers are paying on time, then we know that the receivables included in Aroma's current assets at any point in time should be collected in full within the next 90 days.

The same terminology is used when we talk about the liabilities of a business: trade payables to be paid to suppliers within one year are classified as current liabilities.

The current ratio will be greater than 1 if current assets are greater than current liabilities. Different businesses, though, have different norms; the norm for a particular business depending on the industry sector for that business. In Aroma's case, the ratio is well in excess of 1, at 2.7 at the end of 20X3. We might conclude that Aroma should not have a problem paying its short term liabilities when they are due for payment. One reason, however, the Current Ratio is a crude measure is because the calculation takes no account of the quality of the assets and liabilities.

Let's dig a little deeper. Let's assume that the bank learns that half of Aroma's trade receivables at the end of 20X3 are under dispute because faulty merchandise was shipped to customers. Although these customers are refusing to pay, no provision for bad debts is included in Aroma's financial statements as the finance director remains convinced that the monies due from these customers will be collected in full.

(Be aware that accounting rules require that if a debt is unlikely to be collected, then a business should reflect that fact in its financials. In Aroma's case, the impact of doing so would be an increase in the provision for bad debts expense by up to $1,175 (half of the total receivables of $2,350) and a decrease in the amount of trade receivables by the same amount included in the current assets on the balance sheet).

The trade receivables of $2,350 at the end of 20X3, therefore, include amounts owing from customers complaining about the receipt of faulty merchandise. The quality of this trade receivables number would be regarded as poor by the bank. In this case, using $2,350 in the calculation of the current ratio gives a ratio that looks healthier than it actually is.

The question is this: what will the bank do if it feels that the finance director is overly optimistic about Aroma's ability to collect its trade receivables?

Answer: the bank will make its own independent determination of the extent to which it thinks Aroma will collect its outstanding debts from their customers. The bank will then decide on adjustments that need to be made to the financial numbers provided by Aroma and input these adjustments to its internal credit rating model.

In Aroma's case, the bank will ensure that the current ratio is calculated using a total current assets number that excludes those receivables that are unlikely to be collected. In the worst case, where the bank determines that none of the $1,175 is considered collectible, the Current Ratio calculated would be 1.9 (($4,000 minus $1,175) divided by $1,500) instead of 2.7 for 20X3.

It's important to realise that adjustments made by the bank are only for the purposes of the credit evaluation of Aroma. Whether Aroma updates its own books for these adjustments is a decision for Aroma's finance director.

Another reason why the Current Ratio is a crude measure of short term liquidity is because current assets include amounts that may not be due for payment for up to twelve months. At the same time, current liabilities may include amounts that are due for payment next week.

The big message here is that banks will look behind the numbers in a balance sheet to get a better feel of short term liquidity before deciding whether the liquidity management of the business is in good shape. Banks will always want to assess if there are any potential collection problems relating to receivables on the books of their customers.

2. The Quick Ratio

The calculation of the Quick Ratio is a slight but significant variant of the calculation for the Current Ratio. It is often quite revealing when making an assessment of the short term liquidity position of a business.

Instead of using total current assets, we use total current assets excluding the value of inventory in the calculation. The reason for this is quite straight forward. Inventory, unlike receivables, has a long journey to go before it becomes cash.

Raw material must go through a production process before it becomes finished goods available for sale. The finished goods must then be sold; only then does the business record cash to be received in the future (if a credit sale) or directly receive cash (if a cash sale). Essentially, what we're saying is that inventory is not 'near-cash'.

This is why the quick ratio is viewed as a better calculation of the ability of a business to readily meet its short term liabilities. That said, as the only difference between the Current Ratio and the Quick Ratio is the inclusion/exclusion of the value of inventory in the calculation, the Quick Ratio remains a crude measure of short term liquidity for the same reasons as those highlighted for the Current Ratio.

3. The Leverage Ratio

This is a measure of the extent of debt in a business. You will see that Aroma's level of debt has increased over the last three years: growing from 14% to 167% over a period of three years. This growth in debt may be an issue for a bank. The bank's view will depend on their assessment of whether Aroma can afford the debt; in other words, if Aroma can generate sufficient cash in the future to meet its debt repayments.

4. Interest Cover

Banks like to be comfortable that interest payment obligations will be met by their customers. Interest Cover is the ratio that measures the extent of that comfort. In Aroma's case, Interest Cover decreased to 6 in 20X3 from 8 in 20X2. The absolute level of cover, however, remains healthy and should not be a particular concern to a bank at this time.

5. Fixed Charge Cover

With this ratio a bank is evaluating the ability of your business to pay all their contractual payments. Such payments would include mortgage repayments, lease payments, rental payments and bank interest payments where the consequences of not paying on time could have a severe impact on the business. Payment to some suppliers, on the other hand, may be delayed a week or two with little or no consequence apart from calls requesting payment.

Interest expense is the only "must pay on time" expense in the calculation of Aroma's Fixed Charge Cover. The ratio has fallen from 12.4 in 20X2 to 7.8 in 20X3, a reflection of the fact that more debt was taken on by Aroma in 20X3. The absolute level of cover, however, at 7.8 for 20X3 remains healthy and should not be a concern to a bank.

6. Cash Flow to Total Debt %

Lastly, Cash Flow to Total Debt % gives the bank a sense of how quickly Aroma can make money to settle its debts. In Aroma's case it could, in theory, pay off all its debt in two to three years if it used all its cash flow for that purpose only. Aroma, of course, as a growing business, is more likely to want to reinvest the cash in the business and possibly borrow more to fund a growing working capital requirement.

The calculation, from the bank's perspective, is a measure of the extent of indebtedness relative to Aroma's ability to generate cash. In Aroma's case, the ratio has fallen from 63% at the end of 20X2 to 45% by the end of 20X3. This fall from 63% to 45% reflects the fact that the rate of increase in debt was greater than the rate of increase in Aroma's ability to generate cash.

You will notice that depreciation is added to net income in both the calculation of Fixed Charge Cover and Cash Flow to Total Debt %. The reason for this is because depreciation is a "non-cash" expense that is deducted in arriving at net income. A business does not pay a depreciation expense to anyone; it is actually a "book entry" recorded each year to reflect the use of fixed assets bought by the business. Fixed assets are depreciated over terms that vary from three or four years (for assets like business laptops) to fifty years (for assets like owned business premises). The cash flows relating to these assets took place when the assets were acquired. This is why depreciation is added back to net income before calculating the cash flow ratios.

Other financial ratios that matter

It should come as no surprise that banks, as part of their credit evaluation, also want to understand the operational efficiency and profitability of your business.

Earlier we introduced the term working capital. We said that the amount of working capital in a business is, essentially, the net amount of money that's tied up in certain short term assets and short term liabilities. A business that has

- an efficient customer debt collection process,
- well managed inventory and production systems, and
- a good payment system that takes advantage of credit terms offered by suppliers

is a business that has good control over the management of its working capital; in other words, an operationally efficient business. **The operational efficiency ratios** that a bank reviews include:

- *Days Receivable:* the number of days, on average, your business waits to collect cash from sales to credit customers; the lower the better although very short credit terms may lose business.

- *Days Inventory:* the number of days, on average, your business holds inventory before it is sold; the lower the better providing sales are not lost due to a lack of inventory.

- *Days Payable:* the average number of days credit your business gets from its suppliers; the higher the better unless it means that you have a problem paying your suppliers.

- *Asset Turnover:* a measure of asset efficiency or productivity; Asset Turnover tells us how much sales your business generates for each $1 of assets; the higher the ratio the better.

- *Working Capital Days:* the average number of days that cash is tied up in your business as working capital.

Profitability also matters to a bank: a business cannot survive in the long term if it is not profitable. The **profitability ratios** that a bank reviews include:

- *Gross Income Margin:* a % measure of profitability; the typical margin for a business depends on the type of business and the industry sector that it competes in. Gross Income = Sales less Cost of Goods Sold.
- *Net Income Margin:* a % measure of the net return for a business. Net Income = Gross Income less all other expenses; the higher the Net Income Margin is, the better.
- *Return on Equity (known as ROE):* the higher ROE is the better, unless it is due to an increasing level of debt that the business cannot afford.

The following table shows the formulae used to calculate each of these ratios:

Other financial ratios that matter

Operational Efficiency Ratios

Ratio	Formula
Days Receivable	Average Receivables X 360 / Credit Sales
Days Inventory	Average Inventory X 360 / Cost of Goods Sold
Days Payable	Average Payables X 360 / Credit Purchases
Asset Turnover	Sales / Average Total Assets
Working Capital Days	Days Rec+Days Inv–Days Payable

Profitability Ratios

Ratio	Formula
Gross Income Margin	Gross Income X 100 / Sales
Net Income Margin	Net Income X 100 / Sales
Return on Equity	Net Income X 100 / Average Owners Equity

Before we do any more ratio calculations, there is something that I must highlight regarding the method of calculation. The financial ratio formulas for many of the ratios in the table entitled 'Other financial ratios that matter' require the use of average numbers. Average receivables, for example, is receivables from the balance sheet at the beginning of the year plus the receivables number from the balance sheet at the end of the year. We then divide the result by 2 to get average receivables. Using averages is normally better than simply taking the latest number from the most recent balance sheet.

Although banks do look in the rear view mirror when reviewing your business, it is only done so that they can better assess the future prospects for your business. A bank's focus is on gathering evidence that allows them to make a judgement on where your business is going in the future. One implication of this 'looking to the future' bias is that banks focus more on ratio trends than on the absolute value of a ratio at a point in time. Their interest is in comparing ratios from, say, one quarter to the next and understanding the business reasons for an improving or worsening trend. It follows that variations by different banks in their methods of calculation of some ratios, which are hard coded in their credit rating models, are of little or no consequence. As long as ratios are calculated on a consistent basis, they will normally reveal the same improving or worsening conditions over time. Let's have another look at Aroma's financials:

Aroma's Financial Statements

Income Statement		20X3		20X2		20X1
Sales		**$12,500**		**$7,000**		**$3,000**
Cost of Goods Sold		**8,750**		**4,900**		**2,100**
Gross Income		**3,750**		**2,100**		**900**
Interest expense	250		50		-	
Depreciation	450		220		130	
Other expenses	1,800		1,480		1,370	
Total Expenses		2,500		1,750		1,500
Net Income		**$1,250**		**$350**		**-$600**
Balance Sheet						
Fixed Assets						
Land & Buildings		$1,500		$500		-
Plant, Machinery, Cars		2,500		1,000		650
		4,000		**1,500**		**650**
Current Assets						
Inventory	**1,650**		**750**		**300**	
Trade Receivables	**2,350**		**900**		**350**	
Cash at bank	-		100		300	
	4,000		**1,750**		**950**	
Current Liabilities						
Trade Payables	**1,200**		**600**		**200**	
Short term bank loan	300		-		-	
	1,500		**600**		**200**	
Net Current Assets		2,500		1,150		750
		$6,500		$2,650		$1,400
Financed by						
Paid In Capital		$2,000		$2,000		**$2,000**
Retained Income, 1 Jan	-250		-600		0	
Current year income	1,250		350		-600	
Retained Income, 31 Dec		1,000		-250		-600
Equity (Owners Investment)		**3,000**		**1,750**		**1,400**
Long Term Debt		3,500		900		0
		$6,500		$2,650		$1,400

This time the numbers highlighted in **bold** are those that we use to calculate Aroma's operational efficiency and profitability ratios:

Aroma: Other ratios that matter

	20X3	20X2	20X1
Operational Efficiency Ratios			
Days Receivable	47	32	21
Days Inventory	49	39	26
Days Payable	59	46	26
Asset Turnover	2.2	2.9	1.7
Working Capital Days	37	25	21
Profitability Ratios			
Gross Income Margin	30%	30%	30%
Net Income Margin	10%	5%	-20%
Return on Equity	53%	22%	-35%

1. Days Receivable

Days Receivable is a measure, expressed in number of days, of how long on average the total amount that Aroma's customers owe is outstanding. For the purpose of our calculations, we have assumed that 100% of sales are sales on credit. The calculation for 20X2 is (($350 + $900) divided by 2) multiplied by 360 divided by $7,000 = 32 days. We can see that Days Receivables has been increasing each year since 20X1. This could be bad news, but not necessarily so. We need to know Aroma's customer credit terms before we can decide if there is a potential debt collection problem or not.

If Aroma's customer credit terms are 30 days, you might conclude that debt collection became a problem in 20X3 since receivables were, on average, outstanding for 47 days. On the other hand, it is possible that Aroma has made a conscious decision to give longer credit terms to some of their major customers and this is the reason for the increase to 47 days. If this is the case, then the increase in Days Receivable is the result of a deliberate business decision and not an issue as long as customers actually pay in line with their new credit terms.

Either way, the bank will want to clearly understand the underlying reasons for the increase in the number of days as the knock on effect of Aroma taking longer to collect its receivables is a higher working capital requirement that needs to be financed.

2. Days Inventory

Days Inventory is a measure of how long inventory is sitting in the warehouse before the inventory is used or sold. If raw material, then it's the number of days before it is moved into production. If finished goods for sale, then the number of days before it is sold.

In Aroma's case, the ratio has also been increasing over time from 26 days in 20X1 to 49 days in 20X3. Again, the more money that is tied up in inventory, the greater the financing requirement is.

This may not be a concern for a young growing business that is expanding its product lines and has made a conscious decision to build up its inventory. At some point, however, the expectation would be for the trend in this ratio to stabilise. The use of a reliable inventory management system that optimises the amount of inventory held in the warehouse at any point in time will minimise the working capital finance required.

The calculation for 20X2 is (($300 + $750)/2) multiplied by 360 divided by $4,900 = 39 days.

3. Days Payable

Days Payable is a measure of how many days credit is taken by Aroma before it pays its suppliers for raw materials purchased on credit.

To work this ratio out, we need to know how much material (in Aroma's case, the raw ingredients used to produce its flavourings) was purchased. This information is provided on the second line of the following table:

Aroma's Materials Used in Production

	20X3	20X2	20X1
Opening inventory of materials	$400	$200	$0
Purchases of materials on credit	5,500	3,150	1,400
Materials available for production	5,900	3,350	1,400
Less closing inventory of materials	600	400	200
Materials used in production	$5,300	$2,950	$1,200

The calculation is then straight forward.

For 20X2, it is (($600 + $200) divided by 2) multiplied by 360 divided by $3,150 = 46 days.

As you will see, the length of time that Aroma has been taking to pay its suppliers has increased from 26 days in 20X1 to 59 days in 20X3. It is important to realise that credit from suppliers is a source of finance; it reduces the amount that needs to be otherwise borrowed from a bank for Aroma's working capital needs.

An increase in Days Payable could be good or bad news from a bank's perspective. It is obviously bad news if the underlying reason for the increase in the number of days is because suppliers are demanding payment but Aroma is unable to pay because it is short of cash.

On the other hand, the increase might be due to the fact that suppliers are now giving more generous credit terms to Aroma; in which case the increase is not a concern as this is, effectively, a source of finance.

In Aroma's case, it is clear that the business is expanding quickly. An increasing amount of money is tied up in inventory and receivables. There has also been investment in fixed assets by Aroma. It is possible that some suppliers are overdue for payment. The bank will be quick to work out if this is the case by reviewing these ratios just like we are doing now and then discussing with Aroma's finance manager.

4. Asset Turnover

Asset Turnover is a measure of sales made by Aroma for every $1 of assets. As with all ratios, what's important here is the trend in the ratio, not the absolute number.

In Aroma's case, the trend does not look good. Each $1 in assets in 20X3 only produced $2.20 in sales, whereas in 20X2 each $1 in assets gave $2.90 in sales. Remember, though, that we can never conclude anything from numbers alone.

The reason for the apparent fall in asset efficiency may be because they have invested heavily during 20X2 and 20X3 to expand their production capacity. If this is the case, then the bank will expect to see a higher Asset Turnover ratio (reflecting higher sales from existing production capacity) when they carry out their annual review in 20X4.

5. Working Capital Days

This ratio tells us how long, on average, cash is tied up as working capital in Aroma's business; in other words, how long the cycle is from the time cash is invested by Aroma in inventory to the time when cash is received from Aroma's customers for the sale of goods sold.

In 20X3, Working Capital Days are 47 days + 49 days – 59 days = 37 days. What we see is that Working Capital Days have increased from 21 days to 37 days since 20X1. Aroma's money is now tied up in the business for just over five weeks compared to three weeks in 20X1.

A review of the three ratios used in the calculation of Working Capital Days helps us to work out if this trend is a healthy one or not. Aroma may have made a credit policy decision to offer more generous credit terms to its customers to attract new business. In this case, Days Receivable will increase and this, assuming Days Inventory and Days Payable remain the same, will result in an increase in Working Capital Days. As long as the business can fund the resulting increase in working capital, and there are no problems with collecting payments from customers who buy on credit, this may well be a smart business decision that gives Aroma an edge over its competition.

6. Gross Income Margin

Gross Income Margins vary from business to business. The bank will know what the market norm for your business is and evaluate your financial performance against that norm. For 20X3, Aroma's Gross Income Margin is $3,750 / $12,500 = 30%, the same as for the previous two years.

As we have said before, we must look behind the numbers to understand what's going on. You might think, for instance, that Aroma's Gross Income Margin should improve over time, due to more attractive purchase discounts as a result of ordering in greater quantities from its suppliers. This would result in a lower cost of goods sold per unit and a higher Gross Income Margin.

If one of Aroma's priorities is to build market share it might, however, decide to pass on those higher purchase discounts to its customers by lowering its sales prices. In this case, the Gross Income Margin of 30% would remain the same.

7. Net Income Margin

Net Income Margin measures the net return to the business by taking into account all of Aroma's expenses in generating its sales. In 20X1, Aroma's low level of activity meant that the Gross Income was not sufficient to cover the expenses of the business. A net loss of $600 results in a Net Income Margin of -20%.

The sales growth in 20X2 allowed Aroma to more than cover its expenses and, by the end of 20X3, Aroma had a Net Income Margin of 10%. A bank would conclude that this growth trend is positive and will likely enquire as to how Aroma intends to maintain that growth trend.

8. Return on Equity

Aroma's Return on Equity indicates substantial improvement from -35% in 20X1 to 53% in 20X3. You might be tempted to conclude that (1) this must be good news for the owners of Aroma and (2) what's good for the owners must be good news from the perspective of a bank.

The reality is that the higher Return on Equity could be good or bad news for the owners and from the bank's point of view. It's not possible, in fact, to make any conclusions until a proper analysis is done of what the driving factors are behind the dramatic increase in Return on Equity. Before we do that analysis let's first take a closer look at the Return on Equity Ratio itself.

Return on Equity: what you must know

One of the critical performance measures for a business is Return on Equity. Return on Equity is a calculation of how much, in percentage terms, the owner earns from the investment of his or her capital. The calculation of Return on Equity is Net Income divided by Equity multiplied by 100.

Let's say you start a business by putting in capital of $20,000. And in your first year you make a profit of $4,000. In this case the Return on the $20,000 capital paid in to your business is $4,000 divided by $20,000. Multiply the result by 100 and you get 20%. The Return on Equity = 20%.

Now, let's change the assumption. Let's assume that instead of investing $20,000 of your own money, you only put in $10,000 as paid-in capital and your business borrows the other $10,000. The total amount of funds available to run the business is still $20,000.

Let's assume also that the business must pay interest of 5% each year on the funds borrowed. This means that there is an interest expense each year of $500 (5% multiplied by $10,000). The business profit for the year is now $4,000 minus the $500 interest expense. And that gives us $3,500. Your Return on Equity is now $3,500 divided by the capital that you paid in to your business (which, remember, is now only the

$10,000). Multiply the result by 100 and the Return on Equity is now 35%.

So what's the point? The point is when a business takes on debt, assuming there are no other changes, the Return on Equity increases. In our example, Return on Equity increased from 20% to 35%.

But would a bank see an increase in the Return on Equity from 20% to 35% as a good thing or a bad thing? The fact is if the Return on Equity for your business is increasing over time, a bank does not actually know if it's good news or bad news until it does some analysis. This analysis is easy to do and can be done for any type of business.

To get started on the analysis, the first step is to divide up the Return on Equity ratio into three financial ratios:

- The first ratio is a calculation that measures the **profitability** of your business. The ratio is Net Income divided by Sales multiplied by 100;
- The second ratio is a calculation that is a measure of the **operational efficiency** of your business. The ratio is Sales divided by Average Total Assets (which we know already is the Asset Turnover ratio); and
- The third ratio is a calculation that measures the **extent of debt** in your business. The ratio is Average Total Assets divided by Average Equity.

When we say Return on Equity can be divided up into three ratios, what we mean is that these three ratios, when multiplied together, always give the same answer as the one we get when we calculate Return on Equity as Net Income divided by Average Owners Equity multiplied by 100.

Return on Equity can actually be divided into more than three parts but let's stick with just three parts for now. The easiest way to convey the power of analysis of Return on Equity is to look at an example. So let's revisit Aroma's financial statements once more.

Aroma's Financial Statements

Income Statement		**20X3**		**20X2**		**20X1**
Sales		**$12,500**		**$7,000**		**$3,000**
Cost of Goods Sold		8,750		4,900		2,100
Gross Income		3,750		2,100		900
Interest expense	250		50		-	
Depreciation	450		220		130	
Other expenses	1,800		1,480		1,370	
Total Expenses		2,500		1,750		1,500
Net Income		**$1,250**		**$350**		**-$600**
Balance Sheet						
Fixed Assets						
Land & Buildings		$1,500		$500		-
Plant, Machinery, Cars		2,500		1,000		650
		4,000		**1,500**		**650**
Current Assets						
Inventory	1,650		750		300	
Trade Receivables	2,350		900		350	
Cash at bank	-		100		300	
	4,000		**1,750**		**950**	
Current Liabilities						
Trade Payables	1,200		600		200	
Short term bank loan	300		-		-	
	1,500		600		200	
Net Current Assets		2,500		1,150		750
		$6,500		$2,650		$1,400
Financed by						
Paid In Capital		$2,000		$2,000		**$2,000**
Retained Income, 1 Jan	-250		-600		0	
Current year income	1,250		350		-600	
Retained Income, 31 Dec		1,000		-250		-600
Equity (Owners Investment)		**3,000**		**1,750**		**1,400**
Long Term Debt		3,500		900		0
		$6,500		$2,650		$1,400

Using the numbers now highlighted in **bold**, we can calculate the three financial ratios that we mentioned earlier for each of the three years:

Return on Equity Analysis for Aroma

		20X3	20X2	20X1
A	Net Income X 100 / Sales	10%	5%	-20%
B	Sales / Average Total Assets	2.2	2.9	1.7
C	Average Total Assets / Average Equity	2.4	1.5	1.1
	Return on Equity: **(A X B X C)**	53%	22%	-35%

Net Income divided by Sales for 20X3 is $1,250 divided by $12,500. And when we multiply that result by 100, we get the 10% you see above.

Average Total Assets for 20X3 is: ($4,000 + $4,000 + $1,500 + $1,750) divided by 2 = $5,625. Average Equity for 20X3 is ($3,000 + $1,750) divided by 2 = $2,375.

You can see when we multiply the three financial ratios for each year, we get the Return on Equity for each year. For 20X3, Return on Equity is 10% multiplied by 2.2 multiplied by 2.4 = 53%.

Let's summarise what these ratios are telling us:

- Aroma's **profitability** (Net Income divided by Sales, %) is a positive story improving from -20% in 20X1 to 5% in 20X2 and a further improvement to 10% in 20X3.

- Aroma's **operational efficiency** (measured by Sales divided by Average Total Assets) is, in fact, a ratio that we talked about earlier: Asset Turnover. Sales growth during 20X2 resulted in an improved ratio of $2.90 in sales (20X1: $1.70 in sales) for every $1 in assets. We can tell from looking at the balance sheet that Aroma invested in more machinery in 20X3. It may well be that Aroma has more production capacity than it needed in 20X3; if this is the case, this would explain the lower ratio of $2.20 in sales for every $1 in assets. The expectation would be for this ratio to improve as Aroma's business expands.

- Aroma's **extent of debt** (measured by Average Total Assets divided by Average Equity) has increased each year. We know this because the ratio has increased each year. In 20X1 each $1 of equity was supporting $1.10 of total assets; so there was little debt in 20X1. By 20X3, however, each $1 of equity is supporting $2.40 of total assets; in other words, there is $1.40 of debt for every $1 of equity.

A bank will regard Aroma's improved Return on Equity during the three years as a combination of:

- **Better profitability** (a good sign),
- **Lower efficiency levels** (not a good sign but there may be valid reasons for it that the bank is 'ok' with), and
- **Higher levels of debt in the business** (a bad sign if the business struggles to meet its debt repayment obligations).

Although it's not possible to have a complete understanding by looking at the numbers alone, the analysis of Return on Equity allows a bank to ask some relevant questions about any business.

The beauty of it all is that you can prepare this analysis before you meet your bank and be ready to explain the underlying reasons for the trends in critical ratios. If you and your finance manager are prepared, you will give your bank a positive impression of the financial management of your business, assuming what you say stands up to close scrutiny.

More generally, for any business, here's what we can say:

When the Return on Equity for your business is higher than last quarter or higher than last year because your business is more profitable or more efficient: that's good news.

When the Return on Equity is higher because you have more debt in your business, this may be a concern. It's **not** a concern when the business can afford that level of debt; meaning that your business generates enough incremental cash to pay the higher interest and debt payments when they are due for payment. Otherwise, more debt will be viewed as a potential problem.

What to remember

- ✓ The credit rating for a business depends on the current health of the business as measured by the health of its current liquidity, extent of debt and cash flow.
- ✓ A bank will expect a loss-making or an operationally inefficient business to have plans to improve, and be comfortable that the business has the ability and resources to make such improvements.
- ✓ Banks focus on the trends in financial ratios. They want to assess if the business has improving or worsening trends compared to last year, last quarter or last month.
- ✓ It's not just about crunching numbers. It's also about your vision for the future of your business, your ambition and your commitment that determines how your request for credit stacks up in your bank's mind.
- ✓ Look behind your Return on Equity to understand to what extent change is due to change in profitability, operational efficiency and extent of debt in your business.
- ✓ Better profitability and better operational efficiencies result in a higher Return on Equity. More debt, though, also results in a higher Return on Equity.
- ✓ Good debt is debt that a business can afford; an increase in Return on Equity due to good debt is not a concern. Bad debt is debt that a business cannot afford; an increase in Return on Equity because of bad debt is a concern.

SECRET № 6

HOW A BANK THINKS ABOUT YOUR BUSINESS FORECASTS

How many forecasts do you show to your bank?

Your bank could analyse the financial results for your business until it comes out their ears; and they would still not know if your business can afford the finance that you are asking for today. The reason for this is the same one we talked about earlier: how much your business can afford to borrow today depends on your cash flow forecast tomorrow.

Your business gets the money today when your bank is satisfied that the cash forecasts show that enough extra cash will be made to meet the future loan repayments and your bank considers those cash forecasts to be realistic.

So how many forecasts should you show to your bank? A business should always prepare not one forecast, but two forecasts:

- A **Likely Case** forecast, and
- A **Downside Case** forecast.

A bank tends to start from the position that your **Likely Case** forecast may err on the optimistic side. The purpose of the **Downside Case** forecast is to tell your bank how bad business could be in the next, say, twelve months.

The objective, of course, is to demonstrate to your bank that there is a substantial downside cushion in your business before its ability to meet debt repayments is negatively impacted. The

Downside Case forecast should show that your business can afford the increase in debt. Obviously, the bigger that cushion is after taking account of the downside assumptions in your cash forecasts, the better.

So, let's be clear here. Your bank's attention is on your Downside Case forecast when deciding how much you can afford to borrow. Yes, it's a little more work to do; your bank, though, will appreciate a meaningful analysis of the potential risks in your Likely Case business forecasts.

The actual mechanics of piecing together a Downside Case forecast means thinking hard about the numbers in your Likely Case forecast. Perhaps your business will need to offer more generous credit terms to your customers to keep existing business.

Offering more generous credit terms will mean, though:

- the amount owed by customers at any point in time will be higher, and
- the money tied up in the business will be higher.

Your business would then need to borrow more to fund a decision to offer longer credit terms; how much you need depends on the actual numbers that are in your forecast.

Maybe you are planning a new product launch and in your Likely Case forecast, the assumption is that the new products will be selling three months from now. How comfortable are you with that?

If you think that there could be delays getting the product to market, then your Downside Case forecast should reflect those possible delays.

- Is there a chance that raw material prices could be more than they are priced at in your Likely Case forecast?
- What if projected borrowing costs are higher?
- What if you lose one or two key customers that are expected to place orders for new product?
- What if an employee you consider critical to the success of the product launch leaves?

And so on.

This type of analysis is not an exact science but it allows a bank to get some appreciation of the impact of changing key assumptions on your financing needs. It also, importantly, conveys to a bank that you have thought about downside risks in your business forecasts.

Remember also that a bank keeps a record of your business forecasts. The accuracy of any previous business forecasts provided is something a bank takes into account when evaluating your current forecasts. Overly optimistic forecasts may come back to haunt you later.

Sensitivity analysis: what it is and why it matters

What it is

Sensitivity analysis is fundamental to the process that banks follow in making their lending decisions. We talked earlier about the focus banks have on cash flow forecasts and, in particular, validating those forecasts.

Banks know well that numbers on their own mean nothing; they focus their conversation on how you arrive at your numbers. They want to review with you the assumptions that you made in calculating your forecast numbers. You might be forgiven for thinking that a bank's appetite for analysis is satisfied at this point. For a bank, though, this is only the start.

Even when your forecast assumptions are reasonable, a bank wants to know the impact of changes in those reasonable assumptions. Often the forecast assumptions for a business are not under the control of the business: no ice cream selling business can control the number of bright sunny days there will be in the coming year!

A banks' answer to this inherent uncertainty in a business forecast is to ask for sensitivity analyses for the key assumptions in your forecasts.

What they want to know is how big or small the change is in the forecast cash balance if your forecast product sales volumes are reduced or increased by, say, 5% or 10%: how sensitive your forecast cash position is to changes in your key assumptions.

The impact of changes in key assumptions on forecast cash positions will, obviously, vary from business to business. Sensitivity analysis is simply the re calculation of your existing forecasts by changing key assumptions in order to gauge the impact on your borrowing requirements.

Sensitivity analysis: Why it matters

Changing some assumptions have little impact on the forecast borrowing needs for your business whilst changing other assumptions have a material impact. When you understand your business, you know the forecast assumptions that have a big financial impact on your business. A bank wants to know too.

When a bank approves a credit facility it immediately has a vested interest in the success of your business. It wants to keep its finger on the pulse of your business. And it does so by monitoring your business performance on a regular basis.

To do that effectively, it must know those key assumptions that, if changed, have a material impact on your borrowing needs. This allows them to monitor your credit and, in the worst case for a bank, evaluate the possibility of having to book a provision for possible loan loss.

Sensitivity analysis is not an exact science but it allows a bank to evaluate the impact of potential and actual changes of critical assumptions on its customers financing needs.

Should you be talking to more than one bank?

Would you prefer to have one or two suppliers for the materials you need to run your business? Of course, you'd prefer to have two suppliers; if one of the suppliers goes out of business, tries to overcharge or delivers late, you have the option of picking up the phone and dealing with the other supplier. A bank is no different to any other supplier; banks are in the business of supplying money.

It's not a big deal for a bookkeeper or accountant to prepare financial accounts from two sets of bank statements instead of one. Two bank relationships also give a business the opportunity to sound out two potential banks on its business plan.

There's another reason why more than one banking relationship makes sense. Once a business reaches a certain size, banks normally prefer to avoid being a sole bank. The reason for this is that a sole bank has less flexibility to manage its level of exposure in the case where its customer has no other commercial banking relationship.

It's also worth highlighting that banks tend to have different risk appetites for different types of businesses. Many banks will favour particular business sectors because of the depth of their business knowledge in those sectors. You need to make sure that the bank you are talking with has sufficient risk appetite for your type of business.

However many banks you talk to, you must be prepared to invest time in educating the bank about your business and keeping your bank informed. Give them regular business updates and share not just the good news but also what you are doing to cope with setbacks in your business. That helps build trust over time.

The more a bank understands your business and the more confidence they have in you, the more likely they will stand by you when the going gets rough. You may have to pay more for credit but they will be less likely to leave you in the lurch at the first sign of trouble.

Bankers use the expressions "warm-nosed" and "cold-nosed" when describing their customer relationships. A cold-nosed relationship is, in fact, not a relationship at all. Cold nosed customers tend to run to another bank at the first sign of cheaper pricing.

In contrast, a customer's business in a warm-nosed relationship is well understood by a bank; it's a business relationship that has been nurtured over the years through good and bad times.* In this case, the banker trusts the owners' professional ability and capacity to deliver.

Last but not least, keep in mind that a proactive, experienced business bank manager can make all the difference for a business. Such a bank manager will work with you to help get the finance that you deserve for your business.

** At least, that's the theory. The reality is that many well established businesses have been turned away by banks post 2008. Current times are, unfortunately, far from normal times. The global financial crisis in 2008 did not come about in a matter of months; it came to a slow boil over the previous ten to fifteen years. This decade will, likely, be characterised by a continued squeeze on the amount of total bank credit available.*

What you need to know

✓ Don't think of your business forecasts as just one set of numbers, but as two sets of numbers: a Likely Case forecast and a Downside Case forecast.

✓ A bank will focus on your Downside Case forecast when assessing your business for credit.

✓ Banks want to understand those things that are critical to the success of your business. Help them to help you; give them the information that enables them to write a decent report for internal approval.

✓ Highlight and be prepared to support your key forecast assumptions. Make sure that your key assumptions are reasonable and you are aware of the sensitivity of changes to your key assumptions on the future cash forecasts for your business.

✓ Small changes to key forecast assumptions that result in big changes to your cash needs receive close scrutiny by a bank.

✓ Banks have different risk appetites for different industry sectors. Make sure that you are talking to a bank that has sufficient risk appetite for your business industry.

SECRET №

7

BUILD A COMPELLING CASE FOR FINANCE

How much finance do you actually need?

> The idea that there's a magic number that's the right number for your business to borrow so that you can do all those things you need to do to grow your business is nonsense. This reality can be illustrated by sharing the story of Chris Copper's commodity business.

There's nothing Chris Copper does not know when it comes to metal production and trading. He's an experienced business manager who's seen the ups and downs over the last two decades in commodity prices and the effects on production in the industry. Although his business growth projections tended to be on the cautious side, Copper's bankers always had high confidence in his business acumen. And Chris always delivered on his business forecasts. His business, though, has lost market share to new entrants to the metals sector in recent years. What Chris realises now is that his caution over many years has left him with a profitable but small business in a sector increasingly dominated by big players.

In retrospect, Chris feels he should have pursued business growth more aggressively. The point is this: the amount your business can borrow today depends on how well you can put the money to work growing your business; different growth projections mean different financing needs. It's the growth in your business that will provide the additional cash needed to make the repayments on the borrowings.

There's another consideration that banks bear in mind when approving finance. Many businesses have an amazing capacity to flush money down the toilet; to spend money where it does not really need to be spent. Perfectly viable businesses fail because the money is used unwisely.

Take a business owner with a background in engineering and systems design. The products developed by this business may be great; but if they take twice as long to develop and twice as much in financing because of the owner's desire for perfection in product design, that's a real problem. The marketing effort is just as important as the product design effort. The over spend on product design means that money that should have been spent on the marketing campaign is not available.

This is why banks take time to understand the intended use of the finance and need to be comfortable that the business can be trusted to use the finance for the stated purpose and use it wisely.

What a bank wants to hear

Let's face it, visiting a bank for finance is a bit like going for an interview. You may not like the process but there's no avoiding it if you're looking for finance. And just like an interview, first impressions count. The meeting is not just about whether your numbers add up; it's also very much about You.

Your Business Plan should already have been delivered two or three weeks prior to your meeting with the bank. This gives the bank sufficient time to look at your business proposition and be ready to have a meaningful conversation with you.

The meeting can then properly focus on a discussion of the merits of your business plan and the specific financing requirements rather than just a discussion on the business plan itself. Be prepared to be asked about more than just your numbers:

- How ambitious, hungry and passionate are you to see your business succeed?

- How committed are you?

- Where do you see your business in three or five year's time?

- Why will a prospective customer buy from you?

- What's unique about your product or service offering?

- Where's your competition today? What are they doing and how are they doing it?

- What are your plans to grow your market share?

You must have convincing answers to questions like these to stand half a chance of making the right impression. You must be able to talk about not just how your business is doing but also what's happening in your market.

I know, as well as you do, that bank managers can come up short on visible emotion; they are not likely to jump over their desk and hug you for putting together a great business plan.

Don't be fooled, though! A bank does expect *you* to be passionate about your business. Passion is equated with commitment in a bank's mind; and banks want customers who are committed to their businesses.

This may all seem like stating the obvious. In a fast changing world, though, businesses that may seem promising are often quickly put at risk because of fast changing conditions. We live in an era of continual advances in technology, product development and marketing. Small businesses serving local communities can suddenly find themselves in direct competition with online rivals offering better products at better prices and more choice.

Understanding the current and expected needs of your market and, then, aligning your organisation to offer products and services to meet those needs is something that a bank expects you to have a good handle on. Any suggestion that your business is vulnerable because of competition is not a thought to leave in a bank's mind.

Any business can be classified as:

- a growing business,
- a mature business or
- a declining business.

This classification is a significant factor from a bank's perspective. It should come as no surprise that, all other things being equal, a bank prefers to lend to a growing business. This is simply because a growing business is more likely to generate greater levels of cash flow in the future. A growing business is a safer bet in terms of its potential ability to service and repay a loan approved today. A growing business is also attractive to a bank because its banking business will grow as their customers' business grows.

I'm not saying that a business forecasting little or no growth in the future will never get finance; what I'm saying is if you can come up with some business growth ideas that you expect to have a positive incremental impact on the cash line, you become more desirable in your bank's eyes.

If getting our hands on finance was only a question of knowing how banks think and understanding what they want to hear, we might relax at this point confident that we've cracked the code. There is, however, one other critical step before you make that appointment with your bank.

That critical step is the need to create a compelling business growth story. That growth story must then be crafted into a presentation that clearly conveys what your business is all about: the strengths and weaknesses of your business operation today, the opportunities and threats facing your business, your business growth plans, strategy and financials that support your request for finance. This is obviously not something that you will knock out in a couple of hours; it takes time to put together.

Remember, a compelling growth story helps make a compelling case for finance. A story, on the other hand, about the need for finance to help a declining business or help a mature business through a difficult patch is not likely to be an attractive proposition from a bank's perspective.

You've probably heard it before: if you always do what you've always done, you'll always get what you've always got. We're all creatures of habit. We do things in a certain way that give a result that, most of time, we choose to live with. We also tend to stay focused and spend time on activities that we are comfortable doing.

Many smaller businesses tend to be more comfortable dealing with short term business activities; they spend much of their time dealing with what has to get done in the next few weeks. This is not a criticism. Most small businesses don't find the time to take a step back and think about what they do and how they do it. Their relentless focus is on getting the job done, with little time left to think about how the job gets done.

This short-term focus, though, has a drawback. It tends to result in a business that maintains its current size of operation. Little if any time at all is spent by many businesses figuring out how to actually grow their business.

Figuring out how to improve on what we do, though, is critical. Setting time aside to figure out how to make growth happen with new products or services in new markets is a must. The happy, but not well known, fact is that there are many small businesses with healthy double digit annual growth rates today. There are always business opportunities whether the economy is in good or bad shape.

And when you think about it, it is small businesses that should be able to grow at these double digit rates. Organisations that uually find it more difficult to maintain high growth rates are big established businesses.

There's another reason for setting time aside to figure out how to make growth happen for your business: it's a compelling growth story for your business that will get the attention of a bank and help you get your hands on the money to make your business dreams a reality.

What you want to remember

- ✓ There's no magic number for borrowing that's the right number. The finance that you negotiate reflects your vision for your business, your growth plans and your forecast cash flows.
- ✓ A business can always find projects and seemingly good reasons to spend money. Finance, though, is a limited resource like any other resource; demonstrate that you will spend it wisely.
- ✓ Show the passion and commitment that you have for your business.
- ✓ Be ready to discuss your market, your business plans and your cash flow forecast. Focus your conversation on the ability to service the requested credit facility.
- ✓ A bank always favours a business with a plan for growth over a business asking for finance to just keep its head above water. A compelling growth story helps make a compelling case for finance.

Notes

THE OUTLOOK FOR BANK LENDING

FINANCE FROM ORGANISATIONS OTHER THAN BANKS

FURTHER READING

The outlook for bank lending

> Everyone appreciates the difference between earning $3,000 per month and, say, $6,000 per month. We understand the direct impact that it would have on our lives. We can easily work out how often we can eat out during the month, how much we can put aside for the family holiday, and so on. If that car we'd really like costs $25,000, we can readily decide if we can afford it or not by borrowing and paying back the loan over a number of years. The sizes of such numbers are familiar to us.

For most of us, though, there is a point at which it becomes difficult to appreciate the significance of large numbers.

For example, the news that the US national debt is $17 trillion (www.usdebtclock.org) and rising; or that the UK total national debt is over £1.2 trillion (www.debtbombshell.com) are not easy pieces of financial information to digest.

The impact these numbers have on most of us is little or no different to the impact if these governments were to declare that the numbers were twice as large.

There's simply a point at which most of us just throw our hands up in the air and say it's a big number. As you know, many countries are already at a point where their national debt is out of control.

There's one other group that has had problems managing big numbers: banks. The capacity of banks to lend money depends on the amount of their capital. The more capital banks have the more capacity they have to lend to you and me. Since 2007, however, the losses incurred by financial institutions worldwide are about $2 trillion *(Source: Bloomberg: WDCI)*, another big number.

But wasn't the banking system saved in the Europe and the US with tax pounds, tax euros and tax dollars? True, but it was only saved. Banks only survived collapse as a result of government intervention. Most banks have been unable to grow their lending activities due to lack of capital. Total worldwide loans by banks to non-banks stood at $6.4 trillion at the end of 2007. By June 2011 that number had risen to $6.9 trillion. The latest available data (as of March 2013) discloses that total worldwide loans by banks to non-banks remains at $6.9 trillion. The sad conclusion is that there has been no growth in commercial lending by banks in the last couple of years. *(Source: Bank for International Settlements Quarterly Review, www.bis.org)*.

The fact is that taxpayers' money only prevented banks from going bankrupt. Taxpayers' money handed over to the banks was never going to be a pass through to businesses that needed the cash just as badly as the banks.

The question that really matters is what effect this will have on your business? In the current harsh economic climate, it is clear that the answer is not good news. Small and medium enterprises (SMEs) do fight hard to get finance and many are not successful. For those lucky enough to get finance, they are likely paying more for it.

There is, though, a glimmer of hope. Politicians do realise that small businesses are critical engines for economic growth in the coming years. In some countries, there are already calls for more competition in the small business banking sector as existing high street and community banks continue to fall short in meeting the finance needs of many viable businesses.

More competition in the commercial banking sector would, of course, be good news.

The sooner the better.

Finance from organisations other than banks

It would be a big mistake to think of the high street banks and community banks as the only source of finance. There are many other financial service organisations and intermediaries offering help with various forms of financing. In this section, a few of them are listed.

Government and community sites

www.sba.gov
offers financing programs (loans and grants) from US Federal, State and local governments to help small businesses grow their operations. Also help for starting a business.

www.businesslink.gov.uk
for help in obtaining finance and grants for business in the UK.

www.cdfa.org.uk
the Community Development Finance Association for business funding in UK to start a local community project.
Also **www.findingfinance.org.uk**

Asset based finance sites

www.businessfactors.com
invoice factoring, accounts receivable financing, equipment loans and leasing to business in the US and Canada.

www.bibbyfinancialservices.com
funding solutions for UK based businesses.

www.venture-finance.co.uk
factoring, invoice discounting and asset based lending for UK based businesses.

www.abfa.org.uk
The Asset based Finance Association in the UK for information on discounting and factoring.

Venture Capital & Business Angel sites

www.vcgate.com
a worldwide directory of venture capitalists, angel investors and private investors.

www.angelinvestmentnetwork.co.uk
a site putting business investors and entrepreneurs in touch.

www.bbaa.org.uk
the British Business Angels Association.

www.MiddleEastInvestmentNetwork.com
connecting entrepreneurs with angel investors in the Middle East and internationally.

www.angelsden.co.uk
business funding for entrepreneurs and businesses.

www.venturegiant.com
another place where investors and entrepreneurs meet online.

www.bvca.co.uk
the British Private Equity and Venture Capital Association.

FURTHER READING

How to Prepare a Business Plan

by Edward Blackwell
Published by Kogan Page.

The Definitive Business Plan: The Fast Track to Intelligent Business Planning for Executives and Entrepreneurs

by Richard Stutely
Published by FT Prentice Hall.

Managing by the Numbers

by Chuck Kremer & Ron Rizzuto with John Case
Published by Basic Books.

Brilliant Presentations

by Richard Hall
Published by Pearson Prentice Hall.

Key Management Ratios, The 100+ ratios every manager needs to know

by Ciaran Walsh
Published by FT Prentice Hall

ABOUT THE AUTHOR

David Sparks worked in business banking for over twenty years in the UK, Eastern Europe, and the Middle East. During this time, Sparks held senior management positions in finance and risk management. Subsequently, he established a successful training and consulting business with a particular focus on teaching bank managers how to evaluate business customers for credit.

With the demand for business credit now greater than the available supply and the likelihood of this remaining the case for some years to come, David Sparks offers practical guidance to businesses on presenting their case for finance in more challenging and turbulent economic times.

Email: davidsparks@financeandbanks.com

3 FREE BONUSES WAITING FOR YOU!

As a thank you for buying this book...

FREE BONUS №1

'If only I'd known what they would ask about my business, I wouldn't have stumbled so badly during the meeting...'
Don't let your bank give you any nasty surprises on the day.
Bonus No.1: Yes, I Want A Business Loan! – 107 Questions A Bank Will Ask Before Lending To You.

FREE BONUS №2

Bonus No.2 is a quality MP3 audio recording of this book.

FREE BONUS №3

Your copy of the Excel worksheets that detail all the financial calculations revealed in Secret No.5.

To receive ALL three free bonuses, go to the following web address: **www.financeandbanks.com/3bonuses** where you just need to give your name, email address and proof of purchase to receive all three bonuses TODAY!

P.S: I hate spam as much as you; I will never pass your details to anyone.

David Sparks

Notes

Notes